Original title:

Lush Landscapes and Ocean Tides

Copyright © 2025 Creative Arts Management OÜ

All rights reserved.

Author: Atticus Thornton

ISBN HARDBACK: 978-1-80581-548-8

ISBN PAPERBACK: 978-1-80581-075-9

ISBN EBOOK: 978-1-80581-548-8

## Misty Mountains and Enchanted Waves

Misty peaks with snoozing bears,
A seagull steals my lunch with flair.
Clouds are hats for rocky heads,
Where goats dance on tops of beds.

Waves play tag with sandy toes,
Saltwater tickles, laughter flows.
Fish wear sunglasses, swim in style,
As dolphins flash a toothy smile.

## Serenity in the Curve of a Coastal Trail

A path winds down with twists and bends,
Seagulls gossip, and the fun never ends.
The sun wears a crown, all golden and bright,
While crabs in tuxedos start a dance fight.

Turtles on surfboards catch a cool breeze,
Laughing at humans who trip on their knees.
Footprints in syrup, sticky and sweet,
Each step we take is a comical feat.

## Hidden Valleys in a Sea of Tranquility

Valleys hide treasures, both silly and grand,
Where squirrels host picnics, all perfectly planned.
A wise old owl gives advice on a tree,
"Life's like a dance, just follow the bee!"

Breezes play tag with the grass so tall,
Where daisies giggle and tumble and fall.
Rabbits wear spectacles, reading their maps,
While gophers rehearse for their latest mishaps.

## Tidal Echoes among the Leafy Wilds

Tides whisper secrets to the mossy land,
While otters do yoga, all perfectly planned.
Frogs in bow ties croak our favorite tunes,
As crickets hum softly beneath the old moons.

The wind tells jokes to the swaying trees,
Rustling their leaves like a chorus of bees.
Waves roll in laughter, tickling the shore,
With playful splashes, who could ask for more?

## Twilight's Kaleidoscope of Flora and Foam

In twilight's glow, the flowers giggle,
While waves play tag and the seaweed wiggles.
Butterflies dance with a splashy cheer,
As ocean foam whispers, "I see you, dear!"

The daisies wear hats, quite fashionably,
The crabs hold court, with pomp and glee.
Seagulls swoop down for a daring pastry,
While flip-flops mimic the ground, quite hasty!

A dandelion sneezes, pollen takes flight,
Bubbles in puddles pop with delight.
A starfish winks with a wink so sly,
Taking bets on who can fly!

So gather your friends, it's time to explore,
Where petals and waves both keep scores.
In this realm of humor and trade,
Every breeze brings laughter, unfade!

## Chromatic Dreams in the Sea's Warmth

In sandy realms, all colors collide,
With jellybeans bouncing on each ocean tide.
Octopuses juggle, oh what a scene!
While fish sport sunglasses, looking quite keen!

The coral sings tunes, off-key but proud,
As mermaids giggle, drawing a crowd.
Seashells whisper tales of underwater pranks,
And a lobster starts mooning its oceanic ranks!

Kitesurfers tumble, they're showing great flair,
While dolphins make faces, they really don't care.
Umbrellas are dancing, caught in a breeze,
Painting laughter, with bubbles and ease!

So book your seat on this riot of glee,
Where hues and hilarity flow wild and free.
Join the jubilee, with toes in the sand,
A kaleidoscope of giggles, unplanned!

## **Mellow Tides Wrapped in Greenery**

In a land where seagulls snicker,
And waves roll in like a bad joke,
The grass wears shades of avocado,
While crabs dance like they just awoke.

Shells giggle as they play hide and seek,
Turtles flip-flopping in their shells,
But watch out for the sneaky seaweed,
It pulls your foot and laughs so well!

## The Call of the Shoreline's Heart

Dunes whisper secrets to the breeze,
As flip-flops flop like awkward feet,
Palms wave hello with a sassy tease,
While sunbathers compete in a tan defeat.

A clam pulls a prank, catfishing sand,
Shells gossip about the latest tide,
Sandcastles lean, don't make a stand,
Each wave leaves 'em with nothing to hide!

## Lullabies of the Wild and the Deep

Fish don't sing, but they whisper tales,
Of sailors lost to their own big dreams,
Octopuses juggling in bright scales,
Leave sunburned tourists sipping their creams.

A pelican drops snacks with great flair,
While dolphins play tag in a frothy spree,
They laugh as the fishermen swear,
Nothing's worse than a slippery sea!

## Glistening Shores of Emerald Embrace

The waves wear green like a fancy dress,
As surfers tumble in a giggle spree,
Where sea stars prance with delight, no less,
And jellyfish float like they're sipping tea.

A crab does the cha-cha on the sand,
While kids build castles, digging with glee,
At sunset, the shores turn to a band,
Playing tunes that only the waves can see!

## Serene Valleys Kissing the Coast

In valleys green, the sheep all prance,
They gossip loud, and join a dance.
A seagull swoops, the sheep take flight,
But land on hills, it's quite the sight.

The waves, they crash with a silly sound,
As crabs in tuxedos stroll around.
The daisies giggle in the breeze,
While beetles wear their party fees.

A fisherman sings to a sleepy whale,
Who munches fish with a side of kale.
The sunshine beams, the daisies cheer,
What a wild world filled with good cheer!

So come along when the sun is bright,
Let's skip and hop, from morn till night.
For where the hills and waters play,
Silly adventures start each day!

## Coral Reveries Beneath the Sky

Corals waltz in a vibrant ball,
With starfish applauding, they're having a ball.
The jellyfish float, with grace go by,
While crabs wear hats that are oh-so-high.

Seashells gossip on the sandy floor,
Claiming they're famous, who could ask for more?
A dolphin splashes with a belly flop,
The fish all chuckle, they can't just stop.

The sun sets low, with hues so grand,
As turtles twirl like they've got a band.
Anemones wave in the evening glow,
While seaweed's dancing, putting on a show.

Let's dive beneath this sparkling sea,
Where laughter and joy are wild and free.
Adventure awaits, so bring some cheer,
The ocean's party is finally here!

## **Where Mountains Meet the Majestic Deep**

Mountains poke at the cottony skies,
While gophers play peek-a-boo with sighs.
A moose wears glasses, reads a nice book,
And the creeks are gossiping, so come take a look.

The trees will whisper the silliest tales,
Of adventures with rangers and earthy snails.
Where the rocks are grumpy and the clouds all frown,
A squirrel in a cape doth rule this town.

Down by the shore, the waves try to tease,
While footprints are left by giggling bees.
The raccoons climb high for a star-studded view,
As rabbits in chorus sing praises too!

So let's wander where mountains and ocean unite,
With friends and giggles, it feels just right.
A playful world of curious delight,
Where nature's humor shines so bright!

## **Petals Adrift on a Briny Breeze**

Petals float on a breezy day,
While seagulls squawk in a sassy way.
A boat drifts by, with a friendly wink,
And the waves roll in to steal a drink.

Sunflowers turn to catch the fun,
While daisies giggle at the setting sun.
The boaters dance with a splash and glide,
Just hope their hats don't join the tide!

The breeze will carry the laughter far,
As crabs play music on a clam guitar.
A fish slips by with a wink so sly,
While cacti giggle and birds go high.

So join the joy on this whimsical ride,
With petals and waves as our guide.
In this quirky world where silliness speaks,
Let's frolic and play for days—oh, the peaks!

## Whispers of Earth

In the meadow where grass goes wild,
A cow thinks it's a show-off child,
With a moo that echoes 'round the block,
Stealing thunder from the tickled clock.

Squirrels chatter, not a clue in sight,
Plotting mischief with all their might,
While daisies nod to the bumblebee's tune,
As if they're jiving under a disco moon.

## Heart of Ocean

The waves come crashing with a splashy cheer,
While seagulls squawk, 'What's the deal here?'
An octopus slips in its dance so fine,
Glued to the rhythm of the shoreline line.

Fish flash their scales, like a fashion parade,
Winking at shells, hoping to invade,
Caught in a tangle of seaweed delight,
They party it up from morning till night.

## The Intermingling of Roots and Waves

Roots peek out, holding their breath,
Grumbling softly of old-time death,
While tides tease toes on the sandy floor,
Playing tag with trees just off the shore.

Bananas hang low, quite the lazy bunch,
Chuckling softly at a gopher's crunch,
They gossip about the sun's warm grin,
Racing each other for the best skin.

## Wind-Whipped Folios of Flora and Foam

The wind takes off with a leafy scream,
As flowers blush, caught in a dream,
A daffodil shakes its head with flair,
While cactus stands still, refusing to care.

The foam frolics in bubbles of glee,
Sipping sunshine, counting to three,
Each ripple giggles at a passing boat,
While frogs toss jokes—it's a wholesome note.

## **Jewel Tones beneath a Twilight Sky**

Colors burst forth as the sun sets low,
Playing hide and seek with the night's soft glow,
A parrot squawks, 'What a show!' with delight,
Fluttering promises of a vibrant night.

Stars enjoy gossiping over the breeze,
While crickets play tag with the buzzing bees,
A glowworm doubles as the night's guide,
In this whimsical world where laughter resides.

## Veils of Mist in Verdant Valleys

In valleys where the green grass grows,
A sheep wears glasses, strikes a pose.
The mist drapes low, a sneaky shawl,
While munching on clover, they still look tall.

A squirrel spins tales of what he can see,
Claiming he's the king of the old pine tree.
Yet, as he boasts, he drops his snack,
And all the birds just laugh and clack.

The flowers giggle, they can't keep straight,
As butterflies dance, they twist their fate.
One lands on a cow, what a sight,
That mooing mess turns quite the delight.

As dusk rolls in, the rabbits plot,
A dance-off challenge, they give it a shot.
The fireflies cheer, flashing their light,
In this valley of giggles, all feels just right.

## **Shimmering Seas under Forest Canopies**

Beneath the trees, the waters gleam,
A crab does the cha-cha, or so it would seem.
The waves crash softly, a giggling sound,
As fish hold a concert, quite renowned.

Seagulls squawk tales, they're quite the jest,
Of snagging a snack that got away best.
With each swoop and dive, they'll cackle and tease,
While fishermen wonder, 'Wait, where's my cheese?'

A dolphin leaps, with style and flair,
Wearing a hat, with quite the rare air.
The ocean's a ball, and who's in charge?
The octopus dancing, he's getting quite large!

Under the canopy, shadows prance,
As turtles join in with a wobbly dance.
The kelp provides rhythm, sways side to side,
In this watery world, it's a goofy ride!

## The Interlude of Water and Wood

Where streams meander, trees play tricks,
A raccoon is hiding, planning his flicks.
Raindrops decide to join in on fun,
Spilling like laughter, oh what a run!

A beaver in shades lays back on a log,
While frogs in tuxedos croak like a fog.
Each splash is a giggle, each ripple a joke,
As nature convenes and hatches a hoax.

The willows sway gently, twirling around,
As a snail on a leaf starts zipping, unbound.
The fish in the stream, they wiggle and dance,
While old Mr. Toad tries to give them a chance.

Bubbles rise up, carrying dreams,
The otters are plotting in sunlight beams.
In this playful world, laughter won't cease,
Where every small splash brings delightful peace.

## Emerald Caress at Dusk's Horizon

As the sun dips low, the sky starts to blush,
A hedgehog rolls by, causing a hush.
The grass whispers secrets, soft in their sway,
While squirrels play tag, in a hurried ballet.

Fireflies buzz in, bringing the light,
To dance with the stars, oh what a sight!
Crickets compose, their symphony clear,
While a bear tunes in, with a yawn and a cheer.

A turtle strolls by, taking his time,
Pausing for snacks, oh, so sublime!
The moon rises slowly, hangs like a prize,
As frogs start to croak, serenading the skies.

In emerald greens, the night wears a grin,
As laughter echoes, playful and thin.
With nature in stitches, night carries on,
In this jubilant haven, till the break of dawn.

## Breezes that Brush the Emerald Canopy

The leaves all chat and chortle loud,
While squirrels dance and seem so proud.
A breeze comes by, a cheeky tease,
And tickles toes of playful trees.

The sunlight winks between the boughs,
With butterflies performing vows.
A chipmunk laughs, he takes a leap,
And lands on grass—a little heap.

So next time you take a nature stroll,
Beware of laughter; it's on a roll.
The trees may giggle, birds might cheer,
Nature's humor, perfectly clear.

A parrot jokes upon a perch,
While frogs below begin to lurch.
In this green world, where giggles grow,
Even the flowers seem to glow.

## Forgotten Corners of Wind and Water

In hidden spots where whispers play,
Fish wearing hats swim by all day.
A turtle with a monocle sighs,
As seagulls plot their silly lies.

The crabs perform a secret dance,
With moves so funny, give it a chance!
A jellyfish floats with a big grin,
Saying, "Come join me, let's dive in!"

The waves are ticklish on your toe,
As you wonder where the socklings go.
With each splash, a giggle spills,
Who knew the sea had such great thrills?

In corners where the wild things meet,
You'll find some laughter, oh so sweet.
Forget the laugh track, it's all here,
Nature's sitcom, bring on the cheer!

## Mirthful Melodies of the Forest and Sea

Whales sing songs in a voice so deep,
While trees sway gently, not a peep.
A crab joins in with a clumsy clap,
As dolphins giggle in a happy flap.

The logs take part in a wobbly jig,
While otters bob like a playful gig.
The forest whispers, "Have some fun!"
Join the party, everyone's on the run!

The moon spills light like melted cheese,
While critters dance in the evening breeze.
The symphony of giggles is what we share,
With every note hanging sweet in the air.

So when you stroll where green meets blue,
Listen in close, there's laughter for you.
Nature's music, both wild and free,
Is full of fun—just come see!

## Reflections on Glassy Waters

The lake reflects the sky's big grin,
As frogs in shades of green dive in.
They splash around with a plop and hop,
While turtles chuckle, "Oh, what a drop!"

Clouds float by in their fluffy suits,
With a pun from a bird that never roots.
A fish wears glasses, oh, what a sight!
And smirks as he swims left and right.

The sun giggles as it sets towards night,
Creating sparkles, what a delight!
A duck in socks quacks without care,
While fishes swim, doing flair in the air.

So gaze on waters, mirror-like fine,
Where laughter and mischief entwine.
In every ripple, a joke is spun,
A canvas of fun—let's laugh and run!

## Verdant Whispers of the Shore

The grass tickles my toes with glee,
As I dance like a fool, wild and free.
A crab in a tuxedo scuttles by,
As I wonder if he's headed to a fancy pie.

Seagulls laugh at my floppy hat,
While waves play peek-a-boo, just like a cat.
I wave back, but they splash my face,
In this silly, watery, whimsical place.

Mossy rocks wear a wink of green,
And the wind hums tunes, quite the scene.
Every plant's got a joke to unearth,
While I chuckle along, for all it's worth.

So here I prance, with no care in sight,
In this patch of joy, pure delight.
With laughter and nature's playful embrace,
I find my own silly, happy space.

## **Celestial Colors in Nature's Embrace**

Painted skies sprinkle giggles bright,
Clouds wearing costumes that take flight.
Sunset spills jellybeans all around,
While crickets play music, oh so sound.

A parade of daisies sway in line,
Inviting me in for a glass of sunshine.
While rocks gossip, who'll be the next,
To join the dance, it's quite complex!

The breeze swoops in like a playful kid,
Throwing confetti from a candy lid.
I dive in the colors swirling free,
A rainbow giggle, just for me.

Nature's stage is always so bright,
With wigs that shimmer in morning light.
So let's laugh and twirl in this charming glow,
Where the colors sing, and the jokes overflow.

## Tides Beneath the Emerald Canopy

Beneath the green, a secret tide,
With fish in tuxedos, they swim with pride.
Trees overhead act as beach umbrellas,
While frogs practice their best dance fella.

The water giggles as it flows near,
Tickling the toes of folks filled with cheer.
A dolphin juggles, oh what a sight,
As I cheer him on, it's pure delight!

The roots wear sandals, decorated sprightly,
While leaves whisper jokes, oh so lightly.
A snail slides by in a speedy race,
I'm left in stitches, can't keep up the pace!

Here under canopies, time takes a break,
Laughing with nature, for goodness' sake.
With every wave that dances ashore,
I'm lost in humor, and craving more.

## Symphony of Waves and Wildflowers

A chorus of waves sings a silly tune,
While daisies boogie under the sunlit moon.
The ocean hiccups, a splashy joke,
As I join the party, a happy bloke.

Wildflowers gossip with the gusty breeze,
Switching tales with a giggling tease.
The tide rolls in with a bump and a grin,
As fish practice diving, a shimmering spin.

Butterflies flit with a wink and a nod,
While sunbeams play tag, oh how odd!
Each petal is painted with laughter in mind,
As nature grins wide, oh so kind.

In this patchwork quilt of colors and cheer,
Every giggle feels like music to my ear.
With waves at my feet and flowers in hand,
I sip from the joy of this whimsical band.

## Moonlit Canopies Over Ocean's Embrace

Beneath the bright and winking moon,
A jellyfish plans a disco tune.
Seaweed sways, a groovy dance,
While crabs in tuxedos take a chance.

The stars are laughing, oh what a sight,
As dolphins join the party at night.
With waves that cheer and splash about,
There's no such thing as a night of doubt.

The sand is soft, like a furry bed,
While seagulls joke "Watch this!" ahead.
And mermaids sing their silly songs,
In this ocean realm where joy belongs.

The tide retreats, but not the fun,
For sea stars shine, all dressed up, run!
Under moonlit canopies we play,
As laughter echoes the night away.

## Crescents of Tide and Fern

When tides come in like a friendly cat,
Seashells giggle, "Look at that!"
Sea otters juggling with a glee,
As crabs applaud with great esprit.

The ferns twist and wave, doing the twist,
While fish below say, "Not a chance, we insist!"
A pelican drop-tweets from the sky,
As the ocean chuckles, oh my, oh my!

Flip-flops lie scattered, lost in the spray,
As beach balls bounce and want to play.
There's a beach party brewing, what a sight,
This kerfuffle of merriment feels so right.

In the end, the sun gives a wink,
Declares, "It's time for a cold drink!"
With crescents of joy and nature's cheer,
Each wave brings laughter, year after year.

## Nature's Cloak: Ocean's Breath

A wave rolls in wearing a cloak,
Turns out it's just a seaweed joke.
Splashing about in a watery hug,
Flipping fish just give a shrug.

Oysters gossip about pearls so grand,
While sand crabs plot to start a band.
"Let's make some music, loud and bright!"
Their rhythm's off, but spirits are light.

A grumpy turtle, with a frown to share,
Says, "Why swim fast when slow's more rare?"
The currents laugh, they can't resist,
As sea urchins claim, "We're too cool for this!"

Nature wheezes its breath so wide,
With giggles echoing across the tide.
In this funhouse of underwater cheer,
Each bubble bursts, a new joke draws near.

## Glades Beneath the Celestial Ocean

In glades where daisies meet the tide,
A crab in a top hat goes for a ride.
Butterflies waltz on the breeze of fate,
While snails rehearse for the dance they await.

The sun shines down, a spotlight grand,
As fish throw parties in yellow-sand.
"Just keep swimming," a turtle will boast,
While starfish gather to plan their toast.

The breeze carries laughter from shore to shore,
While seashells gossip, "Did you hear more?"
Mermaids paint with colors so bright,
Creating treasures by day and by night.

In this land where the sky meets the foam,
Every creature feels right at home.
Beneath the celestial light we sway,
In glades of laughter, we join the play.

## A Symphony of Flora and Foam

In gardens where daisies feel quite grand,
The tulips hold concerts, isn't that just planned?
Beneath zany skies where the clouds twist and shout,
The sun tickles petals, they giggle, no doubt.

Seashells do comedy, on a stage made of sand,
With waves acting silly, it's all very planned.
Anemones dance, in their swaying ballet,
While crabs do the cha-cha in the moon's soft array.

And laughter erupts from each bubbling brook,
Where fish tell their stories, the kind you can't book.
As breezes play tricks, tickling trees on the way,
Nature's ensemble puts smiles on display.

So grab a cold drink and join in the cheer,
As flowers and fish joke, bringing laughter near.
With every bright bloom, every splash, every cheer,
This symphony's magic is for all to endear.

## Tranquil Shores of Whispering Leaves

Down by where the soft breezes joke with the trees,
All the leaves are gossiping, "Have you heard the tease?"
Banana peels slip on their own, no regret,
While coconuts laugh till they start to forget.

Turtles in bow ties swim circles of fun,
While seagulls wear sunglasses to soak up the sun.
Flip-flops debate if they're better than shoes,
Where each grain of sand spins tales in bright hues.

The waves roll in rhythm, like rhythm on beat,
In a dance-off with rocks to tap those tiny feet.
A crab with a mic and a shell for a hat,
Sings of his life, oh, how quirky is that!

And there in the distance, a picnic awaits,
With sandwiches chatting, their flavors on dates.
Giggles ensue as they savor their day,
On tranquil shores where the jokes always play.

## **Sunlit Paths through Misty Pines**

Through wooded trails where the shadows play tricks,
The squirrels make acorns into magic sticks.
Each pine tree stands tall, but what's that they hear?
A parrot in shades says, 'Let's all give a cheer!'

Sunbeams come bouncing, with laughter in tow,
While fog wears a coat of light misty glow.
Mice tell their secrets, oh what a surprise,
As butterflies drift with mischief in their eyes.

And rabbits in dance-offs, they leap and they twirl,
While daisies join in with a petal-like swirl.
There's humor in nature, it's plain to behold,
With every sly whisper a joke to be told.

So wander these paths, let your worries unwind,
Where pines whisper secrets to those who are kind.
In sunlight and shadows, where chuckles collide,
Find joy in the journey, let laughter be your guide.

## Harmony of Reef and Rainforest

Under the waves where the sea creatures spin,
A fish wears a crown, it's a riotous win!
While starfish debate if they're stars or just sea,
They twinkle and chuckle, 'Let's just be carefree!'

In jungles of green, the monkeys take flight,
Swinging on vines with giggles in sight.
They wear little hats and they dance to their beat,
As an iguana comments, 'What a fancy treat!'

Corals play fact or bluff with a wink,
While swift currents giggle, 'Don't stop to think!'
With parrots as jesters, the rainforest shakes,
Sharing the laughter that everyone makes.

So dive into chaos, leaping fish in the sun,
Where nature composes her symphony fun.
In harmony's play, find joy intertwined,
Where reef meets rainforest, and laughter's Divine.

## Blooming Shores Woven with Tidal Threads

Upon the shore, the flowers dance,
Joining the waves in their frolicsome prance.
Seagulls squawk, wearing sun hats bright,
Pulling off stunts that are quite the sight.

They sip on juice, with tiny umbrellas,
Sharing the beach with penguin fella's.
With flip-flop fish, and crabs in a band,
Who knew the tides had such a grand plan?

The sun plays tricks on the ocean's back,
Jellyfish giggle in a colorful pack.
Sandcastles rise, but with such a twist,
They melt away, like a magician's mist.

Here's to the shores, a comedy act,
Where sand meets sea, and laughter's the pact.
With waves that whisper, and shells that chime,
In this silly world, we dance in good time.

## Harmony Between Petals and Pulse of the Sea

Petals swirl, caught in a whirl,
Sun-kissed faces start to twirl.
A crab in shades, a starfish on a bike,
Who knew the ocean had this much hype?

Butterflies giggle at the fish's tales,
While pebbles plan their wobbly trails.
The tide's high-five brings an uproarious cheer,
With waves calling out, 'Come and join here!'

Daisies throw shade for a clam's afternoon,
While octopuses jam to a groovy tune.
In this chaotic ballet of flora and foam,
Mother Nature giggles, calling it home.

A waltz of tides, a symphony bright,
A daffodil dreaming of oceanic flight.
Together they sing, in a quirky spree,
Paddling through laughter, wild and free.

**Sculpted by Winds and Tides**

Sculptures of sand wave at the breeze,
While the ocean tickles the laughing trees.
A friendly sun plays peek-a-boo,
Casting shadows of mermaids who swirl like dew.

Kites in the sky compete with the gulls,
As seashells gossip about the best mulls.
A dolphin glides in with daring flair,
To share the waves with a jellyfish pair.

The wind whispers secrets to rocks covered green,
As crabs breakdance, creating the scene.
With every splash, the world takes a turn,
Even the sea stars have lessons to learn.

So come ride the ripples, bring laughter to light,
In a world of wonders, everything's bright.
Together we laugh, forgetting our cares,
As tides craft a story in giggles and glares.

## A Tapestry of Waves and Greenery

Kelp sways like dancers in a grand ball,
While sea critters attempt a conga call.
With dolphins flipping and shells that pop,
Even the seaweed won't let the fun stop!

Above the waves, the clouds chuckle low,
As penguins on surfboards steal the show.
Seashells clink, making cheerful tunes,
While flowers lean in to catch the prunes.

The tide rolls in with a playful shove,
A crab turns pirouettes, it's full of love!
With buttercups giggling on the shore,
Every grain of sand is a laugh to explore.

So join this soirée, where land meets the sea,
In a fiesta of colors, wild and free.
It's mother nature's laughter, bold and bright,
Tales of whimsy in every salt-kissed night.

## Nature's Palette: Green and Blue

The trees wear coats of vibrant green,
A splash of blue where fish have been.
Squirrels dance and steal the show,
While seagulls caw and steal the dough.

Under the sun, all creatures prance,
In puddles, frogs begin to dance.
A turtle slips, goes for a ride,
With jellyfish on the other side.

Wildflowers wink, they're quite the prank,
Bumblebees hum, with no need to tank.
Dandelions puff, like laughter in air,
Making wishes, without a care.

The clouds, they giggle, in fluffy white,
While waves roll in with all their might.
Mother Nature chuckles, her art on display,
Creating giggles in her own special way.

## Cascading Greens, Embracing the Ocean

The hills tumble like a toddler's fall,
With patches of green that never stall.
Kites get tangled in branches up high,
While a goat munches grass, oh my, oh my!

Breezes tease trees, they shimmy and sway,
One cheeky leaf says, 'Let's play all day!'
A clam on the shoreline gives a loud sigh,
'Why must the tide always wave goodbye?'

A raccoon is caught in a snack attack,
His paws covered in crumbs, there's no going back.
The seaweed giggles as fishes zoom by,
While crabs do the cha-cha, oh me, oh my!

Colors blend as the evening wraps tight,
With stars boasting glow in shimmering light.
Nature's a stand-up, with jokes so profound,
In this green and blue stage, humor's abound.

## Currents Carving Celestial Paths

Waves whisper secrets in foamy curls,
As shells gossip tales of sea-faring swirls.
The sand tickles toes, a natural tease,
While dolphins play leapfrog with total ease.

Currents wiggle like a dancer's feet,
Trying to keep up with the playful beat.
A crab, with a top hat, struts on the shore,
Claiming his territory, he'll beg for more.

Seashells gather, having a feast,
'How do we look?' says the tiniest beast.
With barnacles wearing their best bling,
They're ready for the ocean's wild fling.

As night creeps in with stars shining bright,
The waves retell stories of joy and fright.
Humor encased in each rippling play,
Where smiles are oceanic, come join the ballet.

## **Leafy Canopies and Rolling Swells**

Branches extend like inviting arms,
While squirrels chat about their charms.
A woodpecker taps, 'Can you hear my beat?'
As sunlight dances on the forest seat.

Mushrooms gather for a giggling spree,
'Who's the funniest?' says the tallest tree.
Rabbits hop past with a tale so grand,
About the best carrot in all of the land.

Oceans and forests know how to tease,
As breezes tickle, 'Please, don't freeze!'
Creatures all gather, a wild revelry,
Nature's comedy plays, unrestrained, carefree.

With curls of laughter that echo at dusk,
In leafy green realms, adventures we trust.
In every ripple, jump, or swirl,
Life is a hoot in this whimsical world.

## Waves Crashing on Mossy Stones

As the waves play tag with slippery rocks,
They slip and slide, oh what a hoax!
Seagulls cackle, what a scene,
'This ocean life, it's quite a meme!'

The seaweed dances, making a show,
Like they're in a wild, wobbly flow.
Crabs doing the cha-cha, 'Look at me!'
While fish flip-flop, bursting with glee.

A hermit crab struts with style so bold,
In a shell too big, a sight to behold.
The jokes write themselves, it's all quite absurd,
With each splash and dash, the laughter is heard.

So let's raise a toast to the playful spray,
Where sea and stone join in the fray.
Nature's a comedian, full of glee,
In this watery circus, just wait and see!

## Serpentine Vines and Sandy Embrace

Vines twist and twirl in a playful dance,
'Don't get too close, you might lose your pants!'
They tangle around with a mischievous grin,
As I step back, I fear I'll fall in.

Sandy footprints lead straight to a mess,
A startled crab in a bead of distress.
It darts in a panic, oh what a sight,
As I laugh and say, 'You're just not polite!'

Coconuts drop with a comic thud,
Create a ruckus, oh what a flood!
A jellyfish floats, looking quite grand,
Then decides to flop onto the sand.

With a wink and a nod to the wild display,
Nature's comedy show brightens the day.
In the twist of the vines and the blast of the tide,
Laughter is found, swept along for the ride!

## The Secret Life of Tidal Glades

In the hidden realms where the water meanders,
Creatures parade in their wacky standards.
Octopuses juggling with style and finesse,
As they wink and say, 'Isn't this a mess?'

Crabs in tuxedos, all decked to the nines,
Mingle and prance with their flirty designs.
A frog strums a banjo underwater with flair,
'This swamp is the best, come join if you dare!'

Muddy footprints lead to a jolly soiree,
Where fish take a break from their usual play.
With jokes about air and the tides that entwine,
They laugh with the currents, 'Oh aren't we divine?'

So next time you wander, take a peek inside,
Where the glades burst with laughter, and creatures abide.

Each dip and each splash is a reason to cheer,
In the secret lives where giggles reappear!

## **Emerald Isles Adrift in Blue**

Amidst the waves, the emerald pops,
Where gnomes float by on their little hops.
They wave and shout, 'Hey, come join us!'
As a coconut falls, causing great fuss!

Sea turtles gossip, sharing tales of the deep,
'Watch out for pirates, and count your sheep!'
They spin in circles just like whirligigs,
Chasing after shrimp with their wiggly jigs.

Seabirds on stilts strut past like the best,
Wearing tiny hats, they pass the jest.
'It's a fashion show on the high tide stage,
With barnacles shining, it's all the rage!'

The sun dips down, painting hues so bright,
While crabs do the moonwalk, what a delight!
On these floating gems, humor's never done,
In the ocean's embrace, we all share the fun!

## Entwined Roots and Endless Waves

In a forest of giggling green,
Trees dance, jitterbugs, unseen.
Roots tangled like hoses, quite absurd,
Slipping on seaweed, oh how they stirred!

The ocean waves high-five the shore,
Laughing at seagulls that bounce and soar.
Crabs wear sunglasses, think they're so cool,
While starfish form a quirky fishy school.

Pelicans prance with their beaks so wide,
Saying, "Did you see that silly tide?"
Shells giggle softly, they whisper and tease,
As tides tickle toes with splashes, at ease.

All together, they sway in a jive,
While the sand plays games just to feel alive.
Nature's a party, and everyone grins,
In a world where the laughter just never ends.

## Ferns that Sigh with Saltwater Kisses

Ferns on the edge of clumsy green blight,
Whisper to waves, "Man, it's quite a fright!"
Saltwater tickles, they start to giggle,
Then dance in the breeze, oh how they wiggle!

Crabs grumble about their sandy abode,
While boisterous seagulls invest in their code.
"Should we start a band?" one clam roars loud,
While a walrus slips in, far too proud.

The shoreline's a circus, what a funny sight,
With starfish proposing a dance challenge, quite right!
Underwater currents plotting their schemes,
While ferns sigh with joy in their salty dreams.

As the tide rolls back, the ferns jump in glee,
Singing, "Look out, world! Watch us be free!"
In a splashy embrace, they kick up some sand,
Just ferns and the sea—what a whimsical band!

## Coastal Echoes of a Verdant Heart

Echoes of green in a jolly retreat,
Frogs on the rocks dance to nature's beat.
Each squeak and croak is a playful tease,
As ocean waves chuckle, stirring up ease.

The pine trees stand tall with a cheeky grin,
While raccoons do cartwheels, it's wild, let them in!
In a seaside parade, they strut and they show,
Wiggling their tails, putting on quite a show.

The tide brings laughter, the gulls join the jest,
Trying to mimic a dolphin's best quest.
Crustaceans chuckle in their tiny parade,
With shells as their hats, oh, how they've displayed!

By sunset's glow, all creatures unite,
In a dance of delight, under stars shining bright.
Nature's an opera, a comedic delight,
Where laughter and joy swirl, day into night.

## Beneath the Canopy, the Sea Speaks

Beneath the leaves where the sunlight peeks,
Raindrops bounce like goofy cheeks.
Swaying branches share silly secrets,
While ocean whispers through all their regrets.

Tidal waves chuckle, as dolphins dive,
In a twisty ballet, they come alive.
"Did you hear the joke?" the seagulls cry,
"Why did the fish forget how to fly?"

Beneath the canopy, whispers abound,
As laughter erupts from the vibrant ground.
Leaves join the party, a riotous affair,
Shaking their branches, filling the air.

The sea plays a tune, the woods tap along,
Where nature conducts its whimsical song.
In ponds full of giggles, life finds its flow,
As joy wraps around them—ah, what a show!

## The Undercurrents of Green and Blue

The trees are dressed in vibrant hues,
While seabirds gossip in the gentle brews.
A crab in a tux, how dapper he walks,
Cracking jokes with a fish that just squawks.

Oh, the waves dance like they've had too much cheer,
Splashing all over, then hiding in fear.
A turtle wears shades, looking quite cool,
While otters keep stealing the seashells, a fool!

Palm trees sway with a rhythm so bright,
Whispering secrets in the warm evening light.
A hot-air balloon floats with grace in the sky,
Chasing the breeze as it's eager to fly.

But as night falls, a starfish takes the stage,
Reciting bad puns, finding its rage.
The sea joins the laughter, the grass gives a sigh,
In this wacky world where the silly things lie.

## Parables of Paradise and Surf

In the realm where coconuts play the fool,
The surfboards gossip like kids at a school.
A flamingo with flair sings off-key delight,
While dolphins are cracking jokes in clear sight.

The sand is a blanket, so warm and inviting,
Where crabs have a party, their dancing igniting.
A seagull in sunglasses claims he's the king,
While sunbathers laugh, making wishes to spring.

The ocean waves whisper sweet nothings of jest,
As clams do the cha-cha, they think they're the best.
And though the surf's wild, all the critters conspire,
To throw in some pranks that light up the fire.

So, if you drift near where the palm trees sway,
Join in on the silliness, laugh the day away.
For joy thrives where the salty breeze blows,
In this tale of earthly giggles and glows.

## Coral Shadows among Lush Foliage

Beneath the waves, a party starts to bloom,
With sea urchins busting out of their room.
A clown fish tells jokes while juggling seaweed,
While octopuses ponder their next big need.

Coral castles rise with an elegant twist,
As shrimp throw a bash, you won't want to miss.
A lone seahorse pretends he's a knight,
In armor of shells, what a curious sight!

Above water, the ferns join the flair,
While lizards get tangled in sun-soaked hair.
A parrot cracks puns, like a master of jest,
Giving the dragonflies a real run for their fest.

And then there's the breeze, with a giggle it flows,
Tickling the sea, as a wacky show grows.
So dive into fun where the colors collide,
Where creatures engage in their comical stride.

## The Ocean's Whisper in a Forest Glade

In shadows of giants, the tide takes a peek,
As sand crabs and squirrels share ticklish squeaks.
The brook sings a tune with a bubbly embrace,
While turtles attempt to join in the race.

Sunflowers shimmy, and lilies will sway,
Chasing the whispers that float down the way.
A wise old raccoon tries to teach a young hare,
The art of the wave and the dance in the air.

The rocks wear their moss like a hat made of fun,
As laughter erupts when the bubblegum's done.
A woodpecker knocks out a beat on the trees,
While fish poke their heads through to wriggle with glee.

So wander the glade where the weird meets the wild,
In a world where each creature remains just a child.
For whispers of oceans and giggles abound,
In a forest alive with joy all around.

## A Tapestry of Verdant Dreams

In the jungle, vines dance high,
While monkeys argue 'gainst the sky.
A parrot squawked, 'I need a snack!'
But found only a cactus pack.

With shrubs that giggle in the breeze,
And flowers winking at the bees,
The ferns are plotting, so they say,
To have a party—who needs clay?

The hills are rolling, what a sight,
A hill once tripped and took a flight.
The trees are gossiping like folks,
As squirrels crack jokes and tell bad hoax.

Through tangled roots and leafy fray,
The ground seems ticklish, so they play.
As sunlight tickles leaves so bright,
The laughter echoes in delight!

## Ferns and Foam in Quiet Solitude

A sea of greens and frothy waves,
Where crabs write poems in their caves.
The seaweed sways, a dance so grand,
While hermit crabs form a band.

The ferns wave hello with a twist,
While sand dollars talk, just missed.
Starfish giggle, stuck on the shore,
While whales joke beneath the ocean floor.

The tide pools bubble with secret glee,
As otters juggle with a sea spree.
Corals grinning with every brush,
While fish gossip, creating a hush.

A crab in a top hat, what a sight,
As waves blast jokes with all their might.
Nature chuckles, the reefs respond,
Their jokes flowing, ever so fond!

## Waves of Color in Nature's Embrace

In a garden where colors collide,
A butterfly slips for a wild ride.
The tulips gossip in shades so bold,
While daisies share secrets, quietly told.

The ocean sprays laughter, oh what fun,
As seagulls dive and try to run.
With each wave crashing, a comic scene,
The dolphins leap, their humor keen.

Anemones wave with playful glee,
Sardines twirl like they're dancing free.
The sun dips low, a brilliant splash,
As waves high-five, making quite the crash.

In colors bright, the world is spun,
A playful wink from everyone.
They're all in on the cosmic joke,
Nature chuckling as the waves evoke!

## Echoes of the Coast within Canopies

Under the canopy, the birds chirp loud,
As squirrels tumble, feeling proud.
The waves sing songs to trees so tall,
While sea shells chuckle at it all.

A fish once leapt, tripped on a branch,
The octopus tried, but missed its chance.
With whispers of wind and sounds of the sea,
Nature's humor, wild and free.

The branches stretch, trying to reach,
As crabs teach yoga on the beach.
The waves roll in, a friendly tease,
While the grass giggles in the breeze.

With laughter echoing near and far,
The coast is a comedy – oh, how bizarre!
In nature's bowl, merriment blends,
Where land and sea make lighthearted friends!

## Celestial Reflections in Salt and Grass

Beneath the sky, a twinkling dress,
The ocean winks, causing quite the mess.
Seagulls squawk with a curious pout,
"Why bring sandwiches? We're here to scout!"

The grass does sway, like dancers bold,
With shoes of dew, a story told.
Chasing crabs in a tug-of-war,
"It's my lunch! No, it's mine!"—what a score!

Clouds play tag, swift in their flight,
While waves try to steal the starry light.
A splash of salt and a giggling glee,
Nature's joke on you and me.

The sun's upward grin sets up a jest,
As beachgoers vie for the ultimate fest.
With sand in shoes, oh what a plight,
But isn't it grand? This sandy delight!

## Flora's Embrace of the Foamy Edge.

The flowers giggle in the breeze's sway,
While frothy waves come out to play.
A clumsy crab trips over a shell,
"This day is wild! I'm under a spell!"

I found a star—more like a fry!
It winked at me, oh my, oh my!
With petals dancing and sea calling,
Is it me, or is the world just sprawling?

The ocean whispers secrets sweet,
To seashells brave that can feel the beat.
"You've got a shell—so where's your tune?"
Rocks lie back, enjoying the noon.

In a silky dress of waves and grass,
Flora jives, oh, what a sass!
Life's a show on this merry stage,
Let's dance together, let's disengage!

## Emerald Waves Cradle the Shore

Emerald waves with a cheeky grin,
Tug at toes, inviting in.
Fish tell tales in bubbling glee,
"Join us now! Just wait and see!"

The pebbles roll like gossiping friends,
As crabs gossip, the fun never ends.
In bloom, the flowers peek at the tide,
"We're just waiting for Nature to decide!"

A sun hat floats by, caught in a spree,
With sunglasses on, pretending to be.
Perched on seaweed, giggling away,
"Who knew the ocean could make us sway?"

Sandy footprints lead to nowhere fast,
As wind carries chuckles from the past.
In this playful dance, we can't ignore,
Life's a beach—let's just explore!

## **Whispering Pines in Sunset's Glow**

Whispering pines, with secrets to share,
Laughing at sunsets that dance in the air.
The crickets chirp their buggy song,
While shadows stretch and play along.

A squirrel scurries, a nut in tow,
"This stash is mine; you didn't know!"
The sun dips low, a golden tease,
"Where's my drink? I could use a breeze!"

The waves chuckle, kissing the land,
While trees gather round, a merry band.
"Raise your branches, let's give a cheer!
It's sunset o'clock, we've made it here!"

Together they sway, a balmy affair,
Under the glow, without a care.
In this funny dance of dusk and light,
Nature reminds us, everything's right!

## Ebbing Shores of Endless Green

The seaweed wiggles on the sand,
As gulls squawk plans, unplanned.
Turtles race with quite a flair,
While crabs are plotting snacks to share.

The waves recite their salty jokes,
While seashells hum to frolicking folks.
A fish in a tie gives a sly wink,
While barnacles hold their drink!

Seagulls dive, they swoop and swirl,
One steals my hat; oh, what a whirl!
Starfish take selfies on the rocks,
Saying, "Candid shots? We're quite the flocks!"

With each splash, another giggle breaks,
Even the dolphins join in the pranks.
On shores that ebb in charming tease,
I dance with seaweed, oh what a breeze!

## Harmonies of the Earth and Aqua

A squirrel serenades a passing boat,
While frogs compose a woeful note.
The wind gives whispers; grins ensue,
As fish tune up for a Broadway debut!

Rabbits talk about the latest trends,
While raccoons argue on which path extends.
The ocean giggles, the river laughs,
Counting waves like outrageous gaffes.

Seashells clink like glasses in cheer,
"Cheers to seaweed! We love you, dear!"
Footprints dance across the shore,
Tickling a crab that's never a bore!

And when the tide rolls back in shy,
It whispers secrets only I can spy.
With laughter ringing, what a show,
As nature strikes its comedic flow!

## Moonlit Trails through Foliage and Foam

The owls are hooting; a disco night,
While fireflies twinkle, what a delight!
The waves are jiving, splashing around,
Making moonbeams giggle without a sound.

Raccoons play charades in leafy greens,
While turtles check out their moonlit scenes.
Frogs croak tunes in a jazzy beat,
While the ocean sways to their high-knee feet!

While shadows dance, the laughter roams,
In a night of whimsy, the tide finds homes.
A clam joins in with a pearl of wisdom,
"Don't forget to have fun! Here's the system!"

As waves flip secrets to the shore,
The breeze joins in; oh, it's never a bore!
Under the stars, we sway with glee,
In this watery comedy, oh so free!

## Celestial Shores Unfolding Dreams

In twilight hues where silliness swells,
Starlit crabs weave enchanting spells.
Anemones chuckle, "What a bright view!"
As silvery fish plan parties anew!

Sitting on rocks, a catfish in shades
Thinks he's the star, and oh! The parades!
Seashells gossip about seaweed's fame,
While the tides play pranks, what a wild game!

Coconut trees sway with flair on this beach,
While waves make music, oh so elite!
Dancing shadows join in the fun,
"Let's surf to Jupiter before day's done!"

Each splash and twirl tells a joke to the shore,
Making sandcastles a cosmic encore.
With every wave, a dream unfurls,
In this funny paradise where laughter twirls!

## Gentle Caress of Sea and Meadow

Waves slap the shore with a giggly grin,
Grass tickles toes, where do I begin?
Seagulls squawk jokes, they're such little punks,
While daisies dance under the bright sun's funk.

Crabs do the cha-cha, all in a line,
Shells hold secrets, like they're in a vine.
Sandcastles crumble, they just can't resist,
A beach-ball rolls by, who could've guessed?

The wind whispers pranks in a breezy tone,
As trees laugh quietly, they're never alone.
I take off my shoes, oh what a mistake,
Mud squishes between my toes; what a quake!

As sunsets paint skies in colors so bold,
The stars chuckle softly, their jokes never old.
Each wave's a giggle, each breeze a tease,
In this funny paradise, I'm just at ease.

## A Haven Where the Ocean Blooms

Here in the cove, where the sea meets the sand,
Starfish throw parties, at least that's the plan.
Anemones dance, with makeup so bright,
They shimmer and giggle in the sweet daylight.

Turtles in tuxedos swim with great flair,
While dolphins play tag; they haven't a care.
Coral plays hide and seek, under the waves,
While seaweed looks grumpy, just wanting some raves.

The surf's a comedian, splashing with style,
Making kids giggle, oh what a big smile!
Crabs in top hats strut down the pier,
Ballet on the rocks, what a sight, oh dear!

The horizon blushes, as day turns to night,
And waves laugh together, what a joyful sight!
Each shell holds a secret, a story to share,
In this bubbly haven, there's love in the air.

## Nature's Palette on Ocean's Edge

Brushstrokes of emerald, banana boat sails,
Seashells collect stories, like homemade tales.
Seagulls paint the sky with swoops and with dives,
While jellyfish float by, looking for hives.

The horizon giggles in strokes of deep blue,
As kids skedaddle, all sticky with goo.
Pelicans perch, donning hats made of reeds,
While crabs point and laugh at the tangled seaweeds.

Floppy-eared bunnies hop right by the shore,
Winking at fish, they're always wanting more.
The sun hangs a smile, its rays start to tease,
As laughter bursts forth on the warm salty breeze.

At twilight, the colors swirl, laugh, and play,
Mimicking joy from the vibrant day.
The canvas of nature, it tickles my heart,
In this funny wonderland, I'll never depart.

## **Where Cove Meets Canopy**

In a nook where the branches bend to the tide,
Frogs throw a party, on lily pads they glide.
Squirrels in shades, sip acorns on high,
While raccoons in tuxes just coo and sigh.

The breeze cracks a joke; the leaves start to chuckle,
Fish splash their approval, creating auddle.
Earthworms in bow ties do wiggle and flail,
As dragonflies dazzle, their wings never pale.

Sunsets drip honey, as the crickets resound,
Owls in the distance start hooting around.
A turtle in glasses reads poetry slow,
Claiming to know things, just to steal the show.

As shadows grow longer, laughter winds tight,
And leaves whisper secrets throughout the night.
In this cove, my heart does a flip,
Each moment is magic, a giggly trip.

## The Dance of Sand and Sea

The waves jumped high, they did a jig,
While seagulls squawked, dressed up so big.
A crab wore shades, looking quite spry,
As shells rolled by, in a salty sigh.

The beach ball bounced with a joyful cheer,
As kids ran wild without any fear.
But oh! Watch out for that sneaky tide,
It loves to play hide and seek—what a ride!

A flip-flop flew, lost its way to roam,
Dancing solo, far from home.
It spun and twirled with every wave,
A one-shoe wonder, oh how it misbehaved!

The sun set low, like a drunken guy,
Painting the sky while dolphins fly.
With laughter ringing from shore to shore,
The sea sang jokes—who could ask for more?

## **Fronds Bathed in Saltwater Mist**

Palm trees swayed with a chipper grin,
As breezes tickled their leaves, oh what a win!
A coconut fell, took a tumble, a scene,
That left little crabs in a giggling routine.

Bikini-clad mermaids sipped on their drinks,
While fish swam by, giving cheeky winks.
A starfish posed for selfies and fun,
Claiming to be the ocean's number one!

The sands whispered secrets to nearby shells,
While gulls tell tales of their grand hotels.
"Room with a view!" they cawed with glee,
"Just book it fast, we get salty for free!"

As shadows stretched, the sun played peek,
And beach umbrellas began to squeak.
In a world of laughter, the night took a dive,
Echoing joy—it's good to be alive!

## **Celestial Horizons and Verdant Dreams**

Stars twinkled knowing we were undone,
As grasshoppers danced under the moon's fun run.
A raccoon juggled with shells and some slime,
Claiming the prize for the best beach rhyme.

The sky wore purple, an awkward sight,
With crickets chirping, it felt just right.
An octopus waved, all colors so bright,
"Hey landlubbers, did you see my kite?"

As whispers of summer sounded the bell,
The hammock swung like a magic spell.
And fireflies sparkled, a twinkling crew,
Doing dance-offs under the sky's grand view.

With laughter that echoed from shore to shore,
The stars joined in, wanting to explore.
In this cosmic party, where dreams take flight,
A night of humor, oh, what pure delight!

## Tides that Sculpt the Silken Earth

A wave rolled in like a giant's grin,
Turning the beach into a quirky din.
Shells and seaweed began to conspire,
In sandy debates that never tire.

A turtle in shades strolled with such flair,
Waving to gulls in the salty air.
"Do you think I'm slow?" he asked with a grin,
"Just wait 'til I race—watch me begin!"

The tide made sculptures, a wacky scene,
Sand castles topped with a jellyfish queen.
"Oh darling, I'm a sand-tastic sight!"
The ocean chuckled, "You're quite the plight!"

As night unfurled her velvety sleeve,
The laughter echoed, who could believe?
With all the smiles twinkling like pearls,
The cosmos winked at the sea's twisted whirls!

## Serene Shores Dripped in Green

Waves wave hello while seagulls tease,
Sandy toes tickle in the playful breeze.
A crab in a tux, what a formal sight,
Dancing in circles, oh what a delight!

Bright shells are treasures, or so they claim,
But all I find is a seagull's fame.
The ocean's a stage, with actors galore,
And all I do is laugh on the shore!

Starfish are starlets, all dressed so fine,
But the jellyfish? They flop, out of line!
With every splash, a giggle extends,
Nature's comedy that never ends!

So let's toast to the sea and its quirky crew,
With waves as our wine and the sky as our blue.
In this carnival called life, we giggle and cheer,
Painting our moments without any fear!

## The Dance of Ocean and Flora

Coral twirls gently, a vibrant ballet,
While seaweed waltzes, in green and gray.
A fish in a bowtie? Well, who would have known,
In this underwater gala, he's clearly the throne!

Sandcastles tumble, crabs take the ground,
With tiny top hats, they prance all around.
A pirate's old treasure? Just a lost flip-flop,
The sea's little jester, it gives quite a pop!

When the tide comes a-calling, the laughter breaks free,
As the starfish replays the same old goofy spree.
The conch shell is blushing, it's heard all the jokes,
While the octopus giggles with all of its pokes!

So join this parade where the ocean's so bright,
With each splash of humor making everything light.
Nature's got rhythm, yes, that's how it goes,
In this whimsical waltz with a buoyant nose!

## Groves Where the Sea Breathes

Coconuts chuckle, they're quite the wise guys,
While palm trees gossip and mimic the skies.
A parrot named Pete steals a splash of the show,
With jokes guaranteed to land as a pro!

The tide rolls in with a tickle and tease,
Whispering secrets through rustling leaves.
The shoreline erupts into joyous delight,
As crabs juggle shells in their comedic fight!

Dolphins jump high, wearing hats or mayhap,
While fish share a laugh in their bubbly tap.
Each wave sings a tune, a giggle-filled rhyme,
In these playful groves where we dance out of time!

So here we join hands, and let laughter ignite,
When the sea is a friend and the day feels just right.
With sunshine and splashes, let's play till the night,
In this land where the sea breathes, oh what a sight!

## Rippled Dreams on a Sun-Kissed Horizon

The sun wears a smile as it rises so bold,
While waves toss around all their secrets untold.
Flip-flops are flying, a game of lost shoes,
Where toes in the sand go on wild little cruises!

The horizon is winking, a cheeky little tease,
With sunsets that shimmer like a playful breeze.
Salty popcorn clouds pop up in the sky,
And the seagulls' caw sounds like they're saying hi!

Jellybean sunsets, oh the colors they dance,
While the tide does the twist like it's got a romance.
With every wave crashing, laughter unfolds,
As crabs set the rhythm, breaking out in bold!

So here's to the ripples and giggles they send,
Where dreams meet the sea, and the fun has no end.
Let's laugh with the tides, our joyous brigade,
In this world where the sunset is the best escapade!

www.ingramcontent.com/pod-product-compliance
Lightning Source LLC
Chambersburg PA
CBHW072129070526
44585CB00016B/1590